The Keto Diet For Beginners

Your Complete Guide To A Ketogenic Diet & Lose Weight In 4 Weeks Eating Delicious Recipes

Table of Contents

Introduction

Congratulations on downloading your copy of the *The Keto Diet For Beginners: The Complete Beginner's Guide to Burn Fat and to Eat and Feel Healthy*. Thank you for doing so.

The ketogenic diet or keto diet plan – for short - is a low-carbohydrate and high-fat system. It provides satisfactory levels of protein which is similar to other low-carbohydrate diets. It has been called many names including a low-carb diet, keto diet, or a low-carb, high-fat (LCHF) diet. Ketosis is a process that occurs every day, no matter what or how many carbs you consume. The superior keto plan speeds up the process with a standard and safe chemical reaction.

The keto diet reduces your body's carbohydrate intake drastically as it is replaced with fat. Your body goes into ketosis which is a metabolic state making your body burn fat for energy. Your brain can also receive energy—transported as ketones from the liver when fat is exchanged. Your body produces insulin and blood sugar/glucose when you eat foods high in carbohydrates; which as a result, are also lowered on the ketogenic diet.

The plan maintains adequate amounts of protein, so your body can repair and regain a healthy status. The diet will also supply you with the calories needed to keep a healthy weight for your height and age.

The following chapters will provide you with some of the basic guidelines for the keto dieting method. You will also be provided with many delicious recipes for lunch, dinner, or just any time of the day that you are hungry.

There are plenty of books on this subject on the market, thanks again for choosing this one! Every effort was made to ensure it is full of as much useful information as possible. Please enjoy!

Chapter 1: What is a Ketogenic Diet Plan?

The stages of ketosis are better explained within this segment of the book.

The Elements of Ketosis

Ketosis is used to help you drop extra pounds and burn body fat using healthy eating practices. Proteins will fuel your body to burn the fat; which in turn, ketosis will maintain your muscles and make you less hungry.

Your body will remain healthy and work as it should. If you don't consume enough carbs from your food; your cells will begin to burn fat for the necessary energy instead. Your body will switch over to ketosis for its energy source as your cut back on your calories and carbs.

Two elements that occur when your body doesn't need the glucose:

- **The Stage of Lipogenesis:** If there is a sufficient supply of glycogen in your liver and muscles, any excess is converted to fat and stored.

- **The Stage of Glycogenesis:** The excess of glucose converts to glycogen and is stored in the muscles and liver. Research indicates that only about half of your energy used daily can be saved as glycogen.

Your body will have no more food (similar to when you are sleeping) making your body burn the fat to create ketones. Once the ketones break down the fats, which generate fatty acids, they will burn-off in the liver through beta-oxidation.

Thus, when you no longer have a supply of glycogen or glucose, ketosis begins and will use the consumed/stored fat as energy.

The Internet provides you with a keto calculator at "keto-calculator.ankerl.com." You can check your levels when you want to know what essentials your body needs during the course of your dieting plan or afterward. You will document your personal information such as height and weight. The calculator will provide you with the essential math.

How it Works

A ketogenic diet will help you reduce your calorie intake to below the volume of calories your body can expend in one day. Therefore, you need to summon the energy stored in the fat cells to deliver fuel to your muscles.

The keto diet will limit the volume of carbs you consume. A significant portion of your fuel for the day will come from fat converted to ketones. A noticeable deal of fat burning can be achieved on greater calories by sustaining food options used with the ketogenic plan. When you have the protein, carbohydrates, and fat ratio monitored by the diet plan such as shown in this cookbook; you are well on the way to a successful diet strategy.

You will not be over-eating with large portions of protein. You won't eliminate fat or carbs which make it a useful and safe diet plan for fat loss. If you take the approach of eating less, without considering your diet—you will be losing essential minerals and vitamins you need daily—which can result in muscle spasms, fatigue, mental fogginess, hunger, headaches, irritability, insomnia, and emotional depression. You can also lose valuable muscle mass; not just the pounds you intended to drop.

By using the lower carb keto plan, you can reduce your carbohydrates, calorie counts, and nurture your body with the suitable amount of water, meat, eggs, fish, veggies, nuts, as well as high-quality oils which create fat loss minus the unpleasant side effects.

The Process

When the glycerol and fatty acid molecules are released, the ketogenesis process begins, and acetoacetate is produced. The Acetoacetate is converted to two types of ketone units:

- **Acetone:** This is mostly excreted as waste but can also be metabolized into glucose. This is the reason individuals on a ketogenic diet will experience a distinctive smelly breath.
- **Beta-hydroxybutyrate or BHB:** Your muscles will convert the acetoacetate into BHB which will fuel your brain after you have

been on the keto diet for a short time.

Tips to Transition into the Ketogenic Diet

- It is a challenging process when you make a choice to change to a low-carbohydrate lifestyle. It takes a lot of willpower to refuse some sugary treats your family and friends can consume and not gain an ounce of body fat. However, you will be ahead of the game plan by using some of these suggestions. The keto plan works, and you can use it whether you are at home or on-the-go. These are the guidelines:

- **Market Time:** When you go to the supermarket, take your new skills, a grocery list, and search the labels.

- **Control the Kitchen:** One of the easiest ways to stay on your plan is to remove the temptations. Remove the chocolate, candy, bread, pasta, rice, and sugary sodas you have supplied in your kitchen. If you live alone, this is an easy task. It is a bit more challenging if you have a family. The diet will also be useful for them if you plan your meals using some of the recipes included in this book.

- **Count the Carbs:** In today's society, almost every consumable product purchased has the nutrient labeling on the package. Check them before you take them home. Take a bit of extra time when you plan a shopping adventure. It is essential to check the panels on every item to keep the ketosis in line. It might be a complicated process at first, but it is worth the effort.

- **Journalize:** Keep a journal/log of everything you eat. If you cheat, that has to count also. It will be a reminder of your indulgence, but it will help keep you in line. Others may believe you are obsessed with the plan, but it is your health and well-being that you are improving.

Potential Goals Are Reached Through Exercise

Short exercises of approximately 21 minutes daily have been scientifically proven to be more beneficial than longer workouts. With this plan, you can get into shape without a room full of equipment. For many years, trainers believed in sit-ups and push-ups with endless repetitions; forget that also.

When you are pumping away on a stationary bike or treadmill, you are building up the cortisol in your body. It is a stress hormone that usually helps burn fat. However, if you have stressful and lengthy exercises planned, your body will move into a protection mode which will cause storage of fat around your midsection. That is the type of that which can put you at risk for cancer, diabetes, or heart disease.

The type of plan that will work for you is a high-intensity interval training (HIIT) method. You can work-out in short intervals during a lunch break or any part of the day you feel the need to get moving. All you need to get going is some fast feet, and high knee lifts as you perform your exercises. After all, you are trying to push your heart to its maximum, not your biceps.

Cortisol Levels and Exercise

First, you need to understand that cortisol is a hormone which is released from your adrenal gland in response to chemical signs or other stress signals. The release of cortisol in long workouts, such as jogging, and the adverse effects of the release of high doses of cortisol for weight loss are essential elements in your successful program. The hormone creates the fight-or-flight reaction as a result of the additional activity/stress during your workout.

Are You Botching Your Workout Progress?

If the answer to these questions is yes, you are impeding your dietary challenge.

- **Insufficient Fuel:** If you want to make your muscles to improve and lose the weight; you need to eat smart before you exercise. Without the extra energy to burn, your body will begin to use the protein from your muscle because it is readily available.

- **Incorrect Warm-Ups:** The effectiveness of your workout may depend on the way you are warming up. Your muscles need to be suppler because without warming up correctly, you stand more risk of injuries. The short of it is;

your muscles will not be flexible enough which could cause tears.

- **Texting:** If you stop working out; your body will cool down creating a slower metabolism rate. You have to keep going. Phones are best left away from your exercise space.

- **Cell Phones in General:** Leave the phone in the locker, and you won't be tempted to chat or text. You will also be more focused on losing the pounds and becoming healthier, instead of a ringing telephone.

- **Incorrect Exercise Procedures:** You need to be sure you are exercising correctly. Others around you might be doing them wrong. Always pay attention to your teacher whether it is in person or through a book such as this one.

Health Benefits

The ketogenic diet is an excellent plan and aids in some of the following illnesses:

- **Improved Thinking Skills:** Your brain is approximately 60% fat by weight. Therefore, you might become confused as you consume high-fat foods. By increasing your fatty foods intake; you will have better chances to better your mind. It can maintain itself and work at full capacity.

- **Obesity and Overweight People**: Many

individuals exceed what is considered healthy figures when it comes to weight. It is imperative to use the keto diet plan to get started on the right path for weight loss.

- **Acne:** By eating fewer processed foods and less sugar; your insulin levels will be lowered, and the acne should improve.

- **Alzheimer's Disease:** The disease's progression can be slowed and the symptoms reduced with the keto plan.

- **Cancer:** Several types of cancer and slow tumor growths are being treated using the keto diet.

- **Pre-diabetes and Diabetes:** Excess fat is removed with the keto plan, which is what is linked to pre-diabetes, type-2 diabetes, and metabolic syndrome. In one study, insulin sensitivity was improved by 75%. Similar results with type-2 diabetes patients indicated that out of 21 participants, seven were successful in eliminating all of the medications related to diabetes.

- **Epilepsy:** Reductions from seizures have occurred in children who use the ketogenic diet.

- **Gum Disease and Tooth Decay:** The pH balance in your mouth is influenced by sugar intake. Your gum issues could subside after about three months on a keto diet plan. You will be consuming healthier foods.

- **Lower Blood Pressure:** Low-carb diets are an excellent way to reduce your blood pressure. It is advisable to speak with your physician about lowering your meds while on the plan. If you begin to feel dizzy; that is one of the first signs the lack of carbs is working. You are headed in the right direction.

- **Improvement of your Cholesterol Profile:** An arterial buildup is generally associated with the triglyceride and cholesterol levels, which have been proven to improve with the keto diet plan.

- **Joint Pain and Stiffness:** Grain-based foods are eliminated from your diet on the keto plan. It is believed the grains can be one of the biggest causes of pain or chronic illness. After all, it has been said before, "no pain –no grain."

- **Lack of Hunger:** The enormous benefit occurs because fat is naturally more satisfying than just carbs. You just need to wait a little longer to become satiated after a meal. The high-carbs will cause the full-state to last longer.

You are now ready to begin your new way of living a healthier life. Follow the simple guidelines, and you will start to burn the fat!

Chapter 2: Breakfast Goodies

Choose from either a salty or sweet choice to get your day started!

Bacon Hash

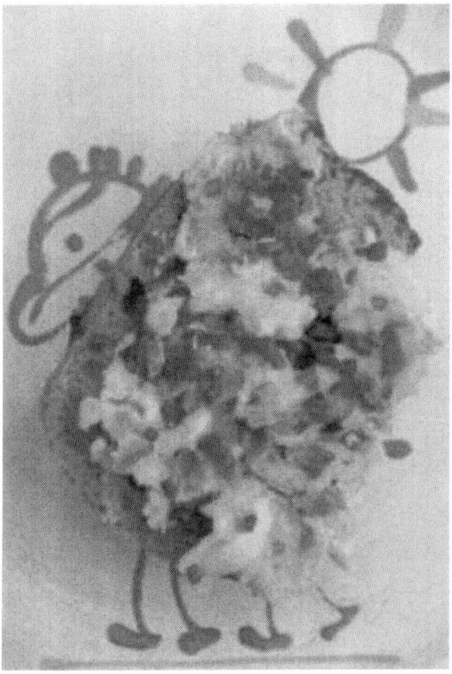

Ingredients

1 small green pepper
Several slices of Jalapenos
1 small onion
4 eggs
6 bacon slices

Instructions

1. Chop the bacon into chunks in a food processor; set aside.
2. Slice the peppers and onions into thin strips and dice the jalapenos as small as possible.
3. Warm up a skillet and fry the veggies. Once browned, combine the fixings and cook until crispy.
4. Place on a serving plate with the eggs.

Yields: 2 Servings (1 serving = 2 eggs)

Calories: 366 | **Protein:** 23 g | **Net Carbs:** 9 g | **Fat:** 24 g

Breakfast Quiche

Ingredients

10 strips of bacon
12 eggs
16 oz. broccoli
8 oz. spinach
1 c. heavy cream
10 oz. grape tomatoes
Pepper – salt -garlic powder: To Taste
5 oz. cheddar cheese

Instructions

1. Set the oven temperature to 375° F.
2. Fry the bacon in a skillet and set aside to drain. Fry the veggies in the drippings and spread into the baking pan.
3. Whisk the cream, eggs, and spices; pour over the vegetables.
4. Crumble the bacon to bits and sprinkle over the top, along with the cheese and tomatoes.

5. Pack firmly and bake for 40 minutes. Sit back and relax.

Yields: 10 Servings

Calories: 313| **Protein:** 17 g | **Net Carbs:** 3 g | **Fat:** 24 g

Philly Cheesesteak Breakfast Wrap

Ingredients

8 ounces deli roast beef/leftover steak – thinly sliced
4 low-carb wraps – ex. Almost Zero (at Wal-Mart)
1 pkg. (½ oz.) 4 sliced button mushrooms
1 oz. - medium bell pepper
½ of a small sliced onion (¼-inch thick)
2 tbsp. olive oil/butter
1 tbsp. Worcestershire sauce
4 oz. (4 slices) Provolone cheese

Instructions

1. Slice the ends off of the peppers, and cut into thin ¼-inch strips. Cut the onion in half and slice into half-rounds, also ¼-inch thick.
2. Warm up a skillet on the stovetop using medium heat. Add the butter and onions,

saute for one to two minutes. Stir in the mushrooms and saute for another two minutes per side, stir around and add the peppers. Cook for an additional one to two minutes.

3. Extinguish the heat and toss in the roast beef/steak along with the Worcestershire sauce. Give it a sprinkle of the salt and pepper.
4. Transfer the mixture to a platter. Add the two wraps to the pan and add the meat mixture. Top them off with a slice of cheese. Cover with foil/lid for about one minute until the cheese melts. It should be ready in about 30 seconds to one minute.
5. Fold them over and enjoy.

Yields: 4 Servings

Calories: 445 | **Protein:** 28 g | **Net Carbs:** 2 g | **Fat:** 32 g

Roasted Mushroom & Cauliflower Grits

Ingredients

6 oz. sliced baby Portobello mushrooms
1 tbsp. of each:
- Rosemary
- Smoked paprika

3 minced garlic cloves
½ c. chopped walnuts
2 tbsp. olive oil
½ c. water
1 med. cauliflower
1 c. of each:
- Half & Half
- Shredded sharp cheddar cheese

To Taste: Salt
2 tbsp. butter

Instructions

1. Warm up the oven to 400° F. Cover a baking tin with aluminum foil.
2. In a small container, mix the smoked paprika, rosemary, walnuts, mushrooms, and garlic. Drizzle with the oil, sprinkle with the salt and toss.
3. Spread the mixture into the prepared pan and roast 15 minutes.
4. Pulse the cauliflower in the processor until fine. In a medium pot, boil ½ cup of the water and add the mock 'grits'/cauliflower. Pour in the Half & Half, and simmer about three minutes using the med-low setting on the stovetop. If you like thinner grits for breakfast, slowly add in ¼ cup of water until you have it the way you want it.
5. Mix in the butter and cheese – heating until well combined and creamy. Sprinkle with salt as desired.
6. When the mushrooms have browned, use them to top off the bowl of hot grits and enjoy.

Yields: 4 Servings

Calories: 455 | **Protein:** 15.28 g | **Net Carbs:** 11.28 g | **Fat:** 36.5 g

Spinach and Mozzarella Frittata

Ingredients

½ onion
1 tbsp. EVOO
1 c. 2% shredded mozzarella cheese - divided
3 egg whites
3 eggs
2 tbsp. 1% milk
¼ t. of each:
-White pepper
-Black pepper
Salt to taste
1 diced Roma tomato
1 cup packed baby spinach
Also Needed 1 slow cooker
For the Pot: Non-stick cooking spray

Instructions

1. Chop and remove the stems from the spinach and dice the onion.
2. Warm up a skillet using the medium setting on the stovetop. Pour in the olive oil, and saute the onion approximately five minutes.
3. Spray the slow cooker with the oil spray.
4. Combine 3/4 of the cheese and the rest of the ingredients in a mixing bowl and add to the slow cooker. Sprinkle the remainder of the cheese on the top of the egg mixture.
5. Secure the lid and cook on the low setting for 1 – 1 ½ hours. The eggs should be set.

Yields: 6 Servings

Calories: 139| **Protein:** 12 g | **Net Carbs:** 4 g | **Fat:** 8 g

Sweets for the Sweet

Pumpkin Bread

Ingredients

1 c. almond flour
1 can Libby's Canned Pumpkin
½ c. of each:
-Coconut flour
-Heavy cream
-Stevia
1 stick melted butter
4 large eggs
1 ½ t. vanilla
½ t. baking powder
2 t. pumpkin spice

Instructions

1. Program the oven temperature setting at 350° F. Grease a pan with some coconut oil.
2. Combine all of the fixings in a mixing container until light and fluffy.
3. Empty the batter into the prepared pan and bake for approximately 70 to 90 minutes.

Yields: 8 Servings

Calories: 311 | **Protein:** 8 g | **Net Carbs:** 5 g | **Fat:** 26 g

Pumpkin Maple Flaxseed Muffins

Ingredients

1 ¼ c. ground flaxseeds
½ tbsp. baking powder
1/3 c. erythritol
1 tbsp. of each:
-Cinnamon
-Pumpkin pie spice
½ t. salt
2 tbsp. coconut oil
1 c. pure pumpkin puree
1 egg
½ t. of each:
-Vanilla extract
-Apple cider vinegar
¼ c. maple syrup
Useful Tool: Blender such as NutriBullet
Garnish: Pumpkin seeds

Instructions

1. Set the oven temperature to 350° F. Prepare a muffin tin (10 muffins) with silicone cupcake liners.
2. Add the seeds to the NutriBullet about one second – no longer or it could become damp.
3. Combine the dry fixings and whisk until well mixed. Add the puree, vanilla extract, and pumpkin spice. Add the maple syrup (1/2 t.) if using.
4. Blend in the oil, egg, and apple cider vinegar. Combine nuts or any other fold-ins of your choice, but remember to add the carbs.
5. Scoop the mixture out by the tablespoonful into the prepared tins. Garnish with some of the pumpkin seeds. Leave a little space at the top so they can rise.
6. Bake approximately 20 minutes. They are ready when they are slightly browned. Let them cool a few minutes and add some ghee/butter or some more syrup.

Yields: 10 Servings

Calories: 120 | **Protein:** 5 g | **Net Carbs:** 2 g | **Fat:** 8.5 g

Pumpkin Spiced French Toast

Ingredients

1 large egg
4 slices *Pumpkin Bread* – recipe previously shown
2 tbsp. cream
1/8 t. orange extract
½ t. vanilla extract
2 tbsp. butter
¼ t. pumpkin pie spice

Instructions

1. Slice the bread and let it dry out overnight in an open-air container.
2. Whisk the pumpkin spice, extracts, and eggs in a mixing dish.
3. Warm up the butter in a skillet until hot, and add the slices of bread. Flip and cook the other side.

4. Serve with some maple syrup and powdered Swerve.

Yields: 2 Servings

Calories: 428 | **Protein:** 12 g | **Net Carbs:** 6.8 g | **Fat:** 37.4 g

Breakfast Pizza Waffles

Ingredients

4 large eggs
3 tbsp. almond flour
4 tbsp. parmesan cheese
1 tbsp. of each:
 -Butter/bacon grease
 -Psyllium husk powder
1 t. of each:
 -Italian seasoning/or your choice of spices
 -Baking powder
Pepper & salt to taste
½ c. tomato sauce
3 oz. cheddar cheese
Optional: Pepperoni

Also Needed

Waffle iron

NutriBullet/blender/immersion blender

Instructions

1. Set the oven temperature to broil and use the blender of choice to combine all of the fixings except for the cheese and tomato sauce.
2. Warm up the iron and pour in ½ of the batter. Repeat with the remainder of the mixture. Add the sauce and cheese on top of each waffle. Add the pepperoni if you choose.
3. Broil for three to five minutes. Lift out and enjoy.

Yields: 2 Servings

Calories: 526| **Protein:** 29 g | **Net Carbs:** 5 g | **Fat:** 41.5 g

Cheesy Thyme Waffles

Ingredients

½ large head riced cauliflower
2 stalks green onion
1 c. of each:
  -Packed collard greens
  -Finely shredded mozzarella cheese
2 large eggs
2 t. freshly chopped thyme
1/3 c. parmesan cheese
1 tbsp. of each:
  -Olive oil
  -Sesame seeds
½ t. of each:
  -Salt
  -Ground black pepper
1 t. garlic powder

Instructions

1. Prepare the cauliflower in a food processor until it reaches a crumbly texture. Toss in the thyme, spring onion, and collard greens – pulsing to combine well.
2. Transfer the mixture to a mixing container, and add the remainder of the fixings, stirring well again. Spoon it over the waffle iron and cook until done.
3. Arrange on a serving dish and enjoy with your favorite toppings.

Yields: 4 Waffles

Calories: 203.25 | **Protein:** 14.99 g | **Fat:** 15.38 g | **Net Carbs:** 5.86 g

Spaghetti Squash Pancakes

Ingredients

10 oz. cooked spaghetti squash
2 eggs
4 slices thick-cut bacon
1 t. of each:
- -Salt
- -Garlic powder
- -Black pepper
- -Onion powder

1 oz. parmesan cheese

Instructions

1. Cook the bacon until crispy, and prepare the spaghetti squash. Reserve the bacon drippings.
2. In a mixing container, add the spices, squash, eggs, and cheese. Blend well, while adding the crumbled bacon.
3. Warm a skillet with the bacon grease and add

the batter to form four pancakes. Compress them flat with the spatula.

4. Brown, flip, and serve.

Yields: 2 Servings (2 pancakes per serving)

Calories: 287 | **Protein:** 19 g | **Net Carbs:** 8 g | **Fat:** 18 g

Chapter 3: Beef – Chicken & Pork Recipes

Beef Recipes

Barbacoa Beef in the Instant Pot

Ingredients

½ med. onion
1 juiced lime
5 garlic cloves
2-4 chipotles in adobo sauce – more or less to taste
1 c. water
1 tbsp. of each:
    -Oregano
    -Ground Cumin
½ t. ground cloves
2 ½ t. kosher salt

Black pepper to taste
1 t. oil
3 bay leaves
3 lb. eye round/bottom round roast

Instructions

1. Set the 'saute' button on the Instant Pot/slow cooker. Cut away the fat from the beef, and slice into three-inch segments. Season with the pepper and salt.
2. In a blender, puree the water, cloves, chipotles, oregano, lime juice, onion, garlic, and cumin.
3. Pour in the oil and brown the meat for about five minutes. Add the sauce (from the blender) and the bay leaves. Cook 65 minutes until it's easily shredded with two forks. Add water if needed to ensure it remains moist.
4. When ready, arrange on a serving platter, shred, and add it back to the pot. Save the juices for later and trash the bay leaves.
5. Measure out 1 ½ cups of the reserved juices, along with ½ teaspoon of the cumin and salt.
6. Serve once it has warmed up and the flavors have blended.

Yields: 9 Servings

Calories: 153 | **Protein:** 24 g | **Net Carbs:** 2 g | **Fat:** 4.5 g

Mexican Lasagna

Ingredients

1 can tomato sauce
2 large zucchinis
½ c. of each:
  -Monterey jack cheese
  -Shredded cheddar cheese
  -Chicken stock
¼ c. of each:
  -Water
  -Apple cider vinegar
½ c. of each:
  -Ricotta cheese
  - Softened cream cheese
1 tbsp. green onions – greens & whites
2 tbsp. of each:
  -Cilantro
  -Extra-virgin olive oil (EVOO)
4 tbsp. taco seasoning
½ lb. ground beef
Optional Topping: Sour cream

Also Needed: 9x9 baking pan

Instructions

1. Set the oven temperature to 375° F.
2. Slice the zucchini lengthwise and into ¼-inch slices. Finely chop the onions.
3. Prepare the sauce in a medium saucepan. Combine the broth, tomato sauce, vinegar, water and two tablespoons of the taco seasoning. Mix well and boil until thickened.
4. Brown the beef in a skillet for approximately five to six minutes. Break it apart and add one tablespoon of the seasoning while the meat is still pink.
5. In another pan, add a drizzle of olive oil and saute the zucchinis for about one minute per side. Add a small amount oil as needed if the skillet becomes dry.
6. Combine the cream cheese, ricotta, and one tablespoon of the taco seasoning and mix well. Spoon in two tablespoons of the taco sauce, and spread it over the bottom of the baking dish.
7. Layer with zucchini slices. Add two tablespoons of the cheese mixture for the next layer. Lastly, sprinkle with the onions and a bit of cheddar cheese.
8. Bake for 20 minutes. Let it cool slightly, slice, and serve. You can also garnish with some sour cream or cilantro (count those carbs).
9. Note: Next time try it with some corn and beans, but add the carbs.

Yields: 4 Servings

Calories: 526.2 | **Protein:** 22 g | **Net Carbs:** 8.3 g | **Fat:** 44.2 g

Spaghetti Squash Lasagna

Ingredients

2 large – cooked – spaghetti squash -approximately 2 ¾ lb.
3 lbs. ground beef
30 slices Mozzarella cheese
1 pkg. (32 oz.) whole milk Ricotta cheese
1 jar (40 oz.) marinara sauce

Instructions

1. Program the oven temperature to 375° F.
2. Slice the squash in half, and put the halves into a casserole dish. Cover the meat portion of the squash with water, and bake for approximately 45 minutes.
3. Brown the beef in a skillet, drain and add the marinara sauce. Set aside once it's warm. Scrape the meat from the squash (the spaghetti), and add to a large baking dish as the first ingredient. Add a layer of meat sauce, mozzarella, Ricotta, and continue until all of

the fixings are mixed in and combined well.
4. Bake for approximately 35 minutes or until the cheese is browned.

Yields: 12 Servings

Calories: 711 | **Protein:** 43 g | **Net Carbs:** 15 g | **Fat:** 59 g

Steak with Mushroom Port Sauce

Ingredients

10 oz. mushrooms
2 oz. heavy cream
1 tbsp. butter
4 oz. port wine
Salt & pepper
2 lb. rib-eye steak

Instructions

1. Preheat the oven to 450° F. Flavor the rib-eye steak with pepper and salt.
2. Add the butter to a cast iron skillet on high. Cook the meat for two minutes per side. Add it to a baking pan in the oven. Cover with foil.
3. For medium rare the internal temperature will be 135° F or a total of 12 minutes, flipping ½ way through the cooking cycle.
4. Pour the wine into the pan to deglaze. Add the cream and mushrooms and cook until

thickened.

Yields: 2 Servings

Calories: 984 | **Protein:** 102 g | **Net Carbs:** 6 g | **Fat:** 62 g

Chicken & Bacon Patties

Ingredients

4 slices of bacon
1 can (12 oz.) chicken breast
2 med. bell peppers
1 large egg
¼ c. of each:
  -Sun-dried tomato pesto
  -Parmesan cheese
3 tbsp. coconut flour

Instructions

1. In the food processor (or by hand), finely chop the peppers and add them to a mixing container. Pat away the excess of liquid.
2. Prepare the bacon – cooking until crispy. Cool

and chop it with the chicken. Add it to the processor until almost smooth. Combine all of the fixings and make patties.

3. Fry on the med-hi to the medium setting in a skillet with a little oil.
4. Once browned on one side, flip it, and continue cooking until done. Let the grease drain on the towels before serving.
5. Garnish with your favorites, but count the carbs.

Yields: 10 Patties

Calories: 95.6| **Protein:** 7.25 g | **Net Carbs:** 1.45 g | **Fat:** 6.16 g

Chicken Korma

Main Ingredient

1 lb. chicken thighs

Ingredients to Blend

1 chopped onion
1 oz. cashews/almonds
5 garlic cloves
½ green jalapeno/serrano/Thai chile pepper
1 t. of each:
- Garam masala
- Salt
- Turmeric

½ t. of each:
- Cayenne pepper
- Ground cumin
- ground coriander

½ c. water (can use to rinse the blender jar & add to the pot)

Ingredients for Finishing

½ c. unsweetened coconut milk
1 t. garam masala
¼ c. chopped cilantro
Also Needed: Instant Pot Slow Cooker/another cooker

Instructions

1. Combine the spices and veggies (blend section). Mix everything together except for the cilantro, coconut milk, and chicken. Add the garam masala last. Pour the sauce into the Instant Pot liner.
2. Add the chicken, and manually program the cooker using the high-pressure setting for ten minutes. Do a natural pressure release and remove the chicken. Chop it into bite-sized pieces.
3. Pour in the milk and garam masala. Transfer back to the pot to warm.
4. Serve when ready and garnish with cilantro if you like.

Yields: 6 Servings

Calories: 256 | **Protein:** 14 g | **Net Carbs:** 6 g | **Fat:**19 g

Keto 'Meatza'

Ingredients

1 can (12 oz.) chicken breast
1 large egg
1 t. of each:
- -Pepper
- -Basil
- -Thyme
- -Garlic
- -Rosemary

½ tbsp. oregano
¾ c. low-carb tomato sauce
1 c. mozzarella cheese
¼ c. parmesan cheese

Instructions

1. Set the oven temperature to 350° F.
2. Mash the chicken thoroughly in a bowl and add the egg. Sprinkle in the spices and cheese. Mix it well until there are no longer any visible streaks of eggs. Adjust the flavor using the spices.
3. Add the mixture to a pizza pan and crush it into the pan with a fork. Toss on the chicken and bake for 15 minutes. When the edges are browned, it will be done.
4. Pour on the sauce, add the cheese, and bake for another 15 minutes.

Yields: 2 Servings

Calories: 446 | **Protein:** 46.07 g | **Net Carbs:** 6.75 g | **Fat:** 25.52 g

Monterey Mug Melt

Ingredients

2 oz. roast beef deli slices
1 ½ tbsp. diced green chiles
1 tbsp. sour cream
1 ½ oz. shredded pepper jack cheese

Instructions

1. Tear apart the roast beef and layer it in the bottom of the dish.
2. First, spread ½ tablespoon of the sour cream, followed by ½ tablespoon of the green chile. Layer ½ ounce of the pepper cheese. Follow with another layer.
3. Microwave for one to two minutes until the cheese melts. Enjoy!

Yields: 1 Serving

Calories: 268| **Protein:** 22.4 g | **Net Carbs:** 3.83 g | **Fat:** 17.99 g

Jamaican Jerk Pork Roast

Ingredients

1 (4 lb.) pork shoulder
1 tbsp. olive oil
½ c. broth/beef stock
¼ c. Jamaican Jerk spice blend (ex. Badia – at Wal-Mart)
Also Needed: Dutch oven

Instructions

1. Rub the roast well with the oil and coat with the Jerk spice blend.
2. Using a Dutch oven, sear the roast on all sides. Add the beef broth. Cover the pot and simmer for about four hours using the low heat setting. You can also bake it in the oven for

three hours at 375° F.

3. Shred and serve.

Yields: 12 Servings – 4 oz. each

Calories: 282| **Protein:** 23 g | **Net Carbs:** 0 g | **Fat:** 20 g

Jerk BBQ Ribs

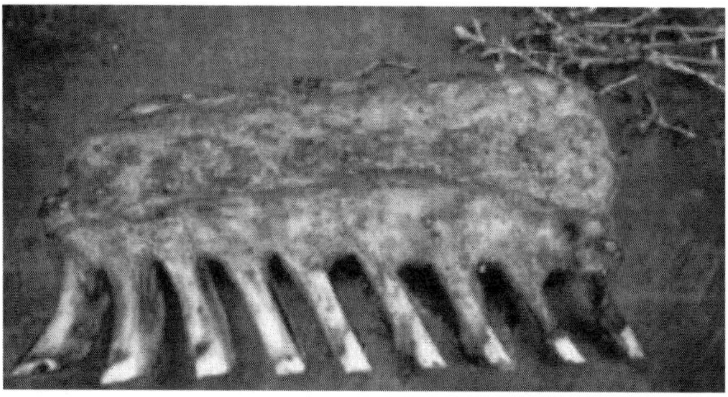

Ingredients

1 c. Caribbean jerk seasonings
1 rack pork ribs (baby-back) – approx. 4 ribs

Ingredients for the Sauce

¼ c. of each:
- -Water
- -Tamari/coconut aminos/soy sauce

2 tbsp. of each:
- -Orange zest
- -Chopped fresh ginger

¼ c. of each:
- -White vinegar
- -Orange juice

1 tbsp. of each:
- -Dijon mustard
- -Worcestershire sauce

2 tbsp. rice wine vinegar
1 t. arrowroot powder/xanthan gum
3 tbsp. sugar substitute

Instructions

1. Warm up the oven to 375° F.
2. Mix the water, tamari/aminos, mustard, ginger, orange juice, orange zest, white vinegar, rice wine vinegar, and Worcestershire sauce in a small saucepan. Once it boils, simmer for approximately eight minutes.
3. Use a strainer to remove the zest and ginger. Pour the sauce back into the pan. Blend in the sweetener of choice and xanthan gum until creamy smooth. Thoroughly cover the ribs with the sauce.
4. Bake for approximately 30 minutes. Let it cool for ten minutes before you slice and serve.

Yields: 6 Servings

Calories: 320 | **Protein:** 34 g | **Net Carbs:** 3 g | **Fat:** 20 g

Stuffed Tenderloin - Keto Style

Ingredients

2 lb. pork tenderloin or venison
½ c. of each:
 -Feta cheese
 -Gorgonzola cheese
1 t. chopped onion
2 tbsp. crushed almonds
2 garlic cloves - minced
½ t. each: Fresh ground black pepper and sea salt

Instructions

1. Preheat the grill.
2. Form a pocket in the tenderloin.
3. Combine the feta and gorgonzola cheese, garlic, almonds, and onions.
4. Stuff the pocket, and seal using a skewer. Grill until you are satisfied with its doneness.

Yields: 8 Servings

Calories: 194 | **Protein:** 28.8 g | **Net Carbs:** 2.9 g | **Fat:** 6.2 g

Chapter 4: Fish & Seafood Recipes

Bacon & Shrimp Risotto

Ingredients

4 slices chopped bacon
2 c. daikon/winter radish/ jicama
2 tbsp. dry white wine
¼ c. chicken stock
1 minced garlic clove
To Taste: Ground pepper
2 tbsp. chopped parsley
4 oz. cooked shrimp

Instructions

1. Peel and slice the daikon/radish, mince the garlic, and chop the bacon. Remove as much water as possible from the daikon once it's shredded.
2. On the stovetop, warm up a saucepan using the medium heat setting. Toss in the bacon

and fry until it's crispy. Leave the drippings in the pan and remove the bacon with a slotted spoon to drain.

3. Add the wine, daikon, salt, pepper, stock, and garlic into the pan and cook six to eight minutes until most of the liquid is absorbed.
4. Fold in the bacon (save a few bits for the topping), and shrimp along with the parsley.
5. Serve and enjoy.
6. Note: If you cannot find the daikon, substitute some shredded cauliflower in its place.

Yields: 2 Servings

Calories: 224 | **Protein:** 23.7 g | **Net Carbs:** 5.3 g | **Fat:** 9.4 g

Coconut Milk & High-Protein Shrimp

Ingredients

1 lb. shrimp (25-30 count to the pound)
½ t. of each:
- -Cayenne pepper
- -Turmeric

1 tbsp. of each:
- -Minced ginger
- -Minced garlic

1 t. of each:
- -Salt
- -Garam masala

½ can unsweetened coconut milk

Instructions

1. Shell and devein the shrimp.
2. Prepare a pan on the stovetop with all of the ingredients.

3. Gently simmer until the shrimp are cooked. Add a bit of extra milk if needed.
4. Enjoy these delicious shrimp with your favorite side dish.

Yields: 4 Servings

Calories: 192| **Protein:** 16 g | **Net Carbs:** 4 g | **Fat:** 12 g

Sardine Stuffed Avocado

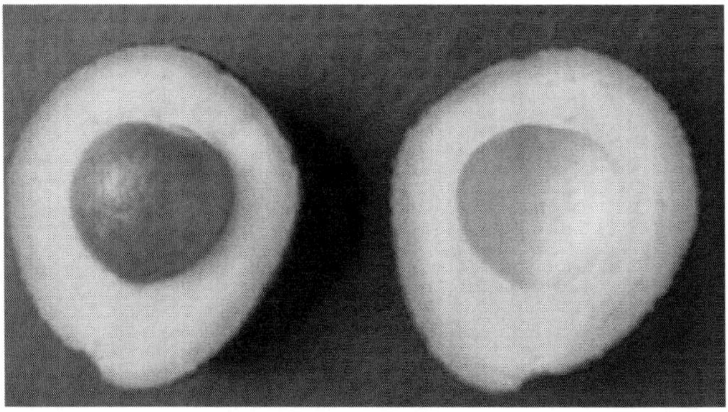

Ingredients

1 tin sardines
1 large avocado
1 med. onion/bunch of chives
1 tbsp. of each:
 -Mayonnaise
 -Freshly squeezed lemon juice
¼ t. of each:
 -Salt (ex. Pink Himalayan)
 -Turmeric powder/1 t. freshly ground turmeric root

Instructions

1. Drain the sardines breaking them into small pieces with a fork. Cut the avocado in half and remove the seeds. Scoop out the center, leaving one-half to one-inch of the flesh.
2. Add the onion, turmeric, onion/chives, and mayonnaise into the sardine dish. Mix in the avocado flesh and give it a squeeze of the

lemon and flavor it with the salt.

3. Scoop the prepared mixture back into the avocado halves and enjoy.

Yields: 1 Serving

Calories: 633 | **Protein:** 27.2 g | **Net Carbs:** 5.5 g | **Fat:** 52.6 g

Chapter 5: Veggies – Soups - Salads & Wrap

Veggies

Broccoli Mashed 'Potatoes'

Ingredients

1 pkg. (12. oz.) broccoli florets
3 tbsp. sour cream
¼ t. of each:
  -Onion powder
  -Garlic powder
2 tbsp. of each:
  -Parmesan cheese

-Heavy whipping cream
Pepper & salt to taste
Also Needed: Immersion blender

Instructions

1. Steam the broccoli in a saucepan for approximately ten minutes.
2. Scoop in the sour cream, spices, cream, and parmesan. Combine with the blender until it is mashed well. Use the low setting to prevent making a puree. You can add a bit of parmesan cheese if it's too thin.

Yields: 4 Servings

Calories: 93 | **Protein:** 4 g | **Net Carbs:** 4.7 g | **Fat:** 6 g

Collard Greens – Southern Style

Ingredients

1 ½ lbs. ham hocks
1 ½ qt. water
4 lb. collard greens
¼ c. vegetable oil
Optional: ½ t. crushed red pepper flakes
To Taste: Pepper & salt

Instructions

1. Prepare a large pot with the water, ham hock, and a tight-fitting top. Once it boils, lower the heat and simmer 30 minutes.
2. Add the pepper flakes and collards – occasionally stirring- for about two hours.
3. Pour in the oil and continue simmering for

another 30 minutes.

Yields: 6 Servings

Calories: 471 | **Protein:** 26.8 g | **Net Carbs:** 17.4 g | **Fat:** 34.3 g

Loaded Cauliflower

Ingredients

1 lb. cauliflower florets
4 oz. sour cream
2 slices cooked bacon bits
1 c. grated cheddar cheese
2 tbsp. snipped chives/other spices
3 tbs. butter
Pepper & salt to your liking
¼ t. garlic powder

Instructions

1. Chop the cauliflower heads into florets and put them in a microwave-safe dish with two tablespoons of water. Cover with plastic film and cook five to eight minutes or until tender.
2. Drain and let rest a minute or two. Squeeze out the excess water. Toss into the food processor and work until fluffy. Add the sour cream, garlic powder, and butter. Process until it looks like mashed potatoes.

3. Scoop into a container and add most of the chives. Work in ½ of the cheddar cheese and sprinkle with the pepper and salt.
4. Top it off with the cheese, rest of the chives, and the bacon. Stick it back in the microwave until the cheese melts or use the oven broiler for several minutes.

Yields: 6 Servings

Calories: 199| **Protein:** 8 g | **Net Carbs:** 5 g | **Fat:** 17 g

Portobello Bun Burgers

Ingredients

1 minced garlic clove
½ tbsp. EVCO
1 t. oregano
2 c. mushroom caps
Pinch of pepper & salt

Ingredients for the Burger Patty

1 tbsp. Dijon mustard
6 oz. organic beef
1 t. salt and black pepper
¼ c. shredded cheddar cheese

Instructions

1. Set the griddle over the high heat setting. Combine the coconut oil and spices in a bowl. Prepare the mushrooms by removing the gills. Add the caps and tops into the marinate until

grill time.

2. Combine the mustard, meat, cheese, pepper, and salt in another dish.
3. Shape the beef into a rounded patty.
4. Arrange the 'buns' on the grill and cook for approximately eight minutes.
5. Add the burger on the grill and cook for about five minutes for each side - until medium rare.
6. Transfer the caps from the marinade dish and assemble the burger.
7. You can also use chicken or turkey to lower the carb/calorie intake.

Yields: 1 Serving

Calories: 668 | **Protein:** 43.6 g | **Net Carbs:** 7.37 g | **Fat:** 52.24 g

Broccoli Cheddar Soup

Ingredients

½ c. chopped med. onion
3 tbsp. ghee/salted butter
1 minced garlic clove
1 lb. broccoli florets (+) more to serve
½ t. dried sage
1 t. salt
2 c. chicken stock
½ c. of each:
  -Whole milk
  -Heavy cream
¼ c. grated parmesan
1 ¼ c. shredded cheddar cheese

To Serve

  -Chopped green onions
  -Bacon bits

Also Needed

-Pressure cooker
-Immersion blender

Instructions

1. Warm up the slow cooker using the saute function and melt the butter.
2. Toss in the onion and saute for about 1 ½ minutes – until translucent. Stir in the garlic and saute for another 30 seconds before adding the sage, salt, and broccoli. Continue stirring approximately every 30 seconds for two minutes.
3. Empty the stock and stir to remove the browning bits from the pot.
4. Secure the lid, sealing the pressure valve and set on the high-pressure setting for two minutes. Quick release the pressure, making sure to be cautious of the steam.
5. Pour in the two kinds of cheese, milk, and cream – stirring well to combine.
6. Lock the lid and set the high pressure until the pressure builds up and quick release again.
7. Use the blender to mix the soup. Pour into bowls and enjoy.

Yields: 8 Servings – ½ cup each

Calories: 209| **Protein:** 8.1 g | **Net Carbs:** 4.4 g | **Fat:** 17 g

Broccoli Cheddar Bacon Chowder

Ingredients

½ large onion
8 bacon slices
2 t. minced garlic
2 tbsp. of each:
- -Butter
- -Coconut flour

½ c. heavy whipping cream
2 c. of each:
- -Low-carb milk (your choice)
- -Cheddar cheese
- -Chicken broth

¼ c. parmesan cheese
4 c. roasted broccoli
½ t. salt
¼ t. cayenne pepper

Instructions

1. Chop the onions and bacon, mince the garlic, and shred the cheddar and parmesan cheese.
2. Prepare the bacon in a skillet using the medium heat setting. Let it drain on towels, reserving approximately three tablespoons of the drippings. Add the butter and saute the garlic and onions for four to five minutes.
3. Sprinkle in the flour and stir for one minute.
4. Pour in the milk and cream together. Add to the mixture in ¼ segments until it starts bubbling. Stir and lower the heat to med-low. Blend in the cheeses and mix well. Simmer for two to three minutes, add the broccoli, and simmer another two to three more minutes. Fold in the bacon and let it cook for about five minutes.
5. Blend until chunky and add the cayenne and broth. Stir and simmer 20 to 30 more minutes – stirring at five-minute intervals.
6. Serve and relax.

Yields: 6 Servings – ¾ c. each

Calories: 476.83| **Protein:** 20.06 g | **Net Carbs:** 7.99 g | **Fat:** 40.41 g

Charred Veggie Fried Goat Cheese Salad

Ingredients

4 oz. goat cheese
2 tbsp. of each:
 -Sesame seeds
 -Poppy seeds
1 t. of each:
 -Garlic flakes
 -Onion flakes
1 med. red bell pepper
4 c. arugula
½ c. baby Portobello mushrooms
1 tbsp. avocado oil

Instructions

1. Chop the cheese into 4 (1/2-inch) medallions. Remove the seeds from the pepper and slice into eight sections. Also, slice the mushrooms.

Prepare two dishes of arugula.

2. In a small container; mix the garlic flakes, onion, along with the sesame and poppy seeds. Coat the cheese on each side, and place in the fridge until ready to use.
3. Warm up a skillet on the stove and add some nonstick spray to it to prevent sticking using the medium heat setting. Char the mushrooms and peppers until browned and add to the arugula dishes.
4. Put the goat cheese in the pan, frying each side for 30 seconds.
5. Gently take the cheese out of the pan, and add it to the salad. Give it a drizzle of the oil and enjoy!

Yields: 2 Servings

Calories: 350 | **Protein:** 16.09g | **Net Carbs:** 7.08 g | **Fat:** 27.61 g

Mackerel Salad

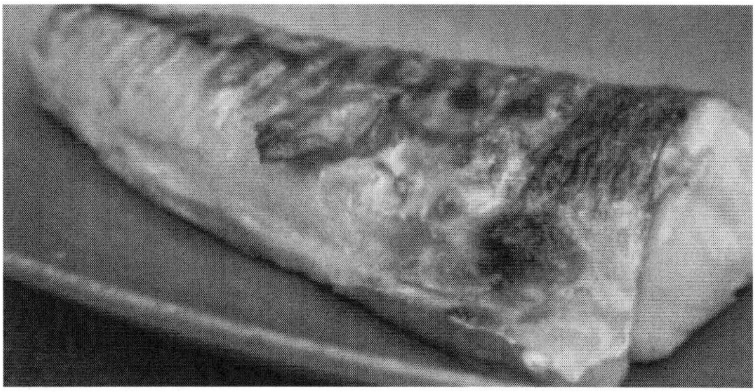

Ingredients

2 large eggs
2 mackerel fillets (6.3 oz.)
1 med. avocado (5.3 oz.)
4 c. mixed lettuce – ex. Arugula/lamb (4.2 oz.)
2 c. green beans (7.1 oz.)
1 tbsp. coconut oil/ghee
Freshly cracked black pepper
¼ t. salt – ex. Pink Himalayan

Lemon & Mustard Dressing

1 t. Dijon mustard – your choice
2 tbsp. of each:
    -Lemon juice – approx. ½ lemon
    -Extra-virgin olive oil

Instructions

1. Prepare the Eggs: Add salt and water to a pan and fill it approximately ¾ full of water. Once it starts to boil, gently add the eggs. Boil 10

minutes. Transfer them to a cold-water bath.

2. Cook the Beans: Season a pan of water with salt, and cook the beans for about four to five minutes. Transfer them to a dish and pour out the water right away to prevent overcooking.
3. Prepare the Fish: Cut small - diagonal - shallow slashes on the skin of each mackerel using a sharp knife. Season with a shake of the pepper and salt.
4. Place a skillet on a burner over med-hi heat. Pour the oil and wait until it's hot. Add the fillets skin side down. The meat will be opaque with a crispy skin. Set on a platter or other container.
5. Make the Dressing: Whisk all of the dressing fixings.
6. Peel the shells off of the eggs once chilled. Slice them into slender quarters.
7. Rinse and drain the lettuce using a paper towel/salad spinner.
8. Arrange the lettuce in a serving dish, and top it off with the prepared beans.
9. Add the fish and dressing on the side and enjoy.

Yields: 2 Servings

Calories: 609 | **Protein:** 27.3 g | **Net Carbs:** 7.6 g | **Fat:** 49.9 g

Mixed Green Spring Salad with 5-Minute Vinaigrette

Ingredients

3 tbsp. roasted pine nuts
2 oz. mixed greens
2 bacon slices
2 tbsp. of each:
- -5-Minute Raspberry Vinaigrette
- -Shaved parmesan

Pepper and salt – to your liking

Instructions

1. Cook the bacon in a skillet until browned and crispy. Crumble and add it to the rest of the fixings.
2. Mix or shake the dressing and add it to the prepared salad.
3. Smile and enjoy!

Yields: 1 Serving

5-Minute Vinaigrette

(Recipe in the sauce section)

Yields: 1 ½ c. Servings – 2 tbsp. each

Calories: 84 | **Protein:** 0.06 g | **Net Carbs:** 0.29 g | **Fat:** 9.03 g

Salmon Salad

Ingredients for the Salmon

2 fillets (8 oz.) salmon
Dash of freshly cracked ground pepper
Pinch Himalayan salt

Ingredients for the Salad

1 tomato
½ English cucumber
2 green onions
4 celery sticks

Ingredients for the Dressing

1 garlic clove
¾ t. of each:
 -Fresh thyme leaves (4 bunches)
 -Fresh rosemary leaves (2 sprigs)
1 t. black mustard seeds
¼ t. sea salt
Pinch of ground black pepper

2 tbsp. of each:
-Fresh lemon juice
-Gluten-free Dijon mustard
-Olive oil (EVOO)
-Water
¼ c. flat leaf parsley

Instructions

1. Slice the cucumber in half lengthwise, then slice again. Dice the celery and tomatoes. Also, finely chop the onions. Roughly chop the parsley.
2. Prepare the oven broiler and cover a baking sheet with aluminum foil.
3. Arrange the salmon on the foil and coat with the pepper and salt. Broil for four to five inches from the heat - based on ten minutes per inch of thickness. Remove when the top has browned.
4. You can choose to serve the salmon on the side. You can also cool and break apart in a large salad dish. Toss in the onions, cucumber, celery, and tomatoes. Set to the side for now.
5. Combine the dressing fixings in a blender/food processor until smooth. Empty over the salad. Sprinkle with the mustard seeds and freshly chopped parsley.
6. Serve and enjoy on the bed of greens or as a sandwich filling.
7. Note: You need to use extra-virgin olive oil and gluten-free mustard for this one to be perfect.

Yields: 4 Servings

Calories: 320 | **Protein:** 26.4 g | **Net Carbs:** 3.5 g | **Fat:** 21.5 g

1 Wrap

Coleslaw-Stuffed Wraps

Ingredients

½ c. green onions
3 c. red cabbage
¾ c. mayonnaise
2 t. apple cider vinegar
¼ t. sea salt

Wraps and Other Fillings

1 lb. regular ground beef/turkey/chicken/pork – cooked & chilled
16 collard leaves
1/3 c. packed alfalfa sprouts
Toothpicks

Instructions

1. Remove the stems from the collards and dice the onions. Thinly slice the cabbage. Add all of the fixings in a large mixing container and stir; stirring well.

2. Add a spoonful of the coleslaw on the far edge of the first collard leaf (the side that hasn't been cut). Add the meat and the sprouts.
3. Roll and tuck the sides and insert toothpicks at an angle to hold them together. Continue until all are done.
4. Sit down and relax.

Yields: 16 Wraps/4 Servings

Calories: 609 | **Protein:** 32.7 g | **Net Carbs:** 3.1 g | **Fat:** 50 g

Chapter 6: Other Main Meals

Cheese-Stuffed Bacon-Wrapped Hot Dogs

Ingredients

12 bacon slices
6 large beef hot dogs
½ t. of each powder:
- -Onion
- -Garlic

Pepper & salt - to taste
2 oz. cheddar cheese

Instructions

1. Program the oven setting to 400° F.
2. Slit each of the dogs and insert the cheese.
3. Wrap the hot dogs with two bacon slices each and secure with a toothpick.
4. Add all of the seasonings to a dish, and roll the dogs through it. Bake 35-40 minutes.

5. Serve and enjoy with your favorite sides.

Yields: 6 Servings

Calories: 283 | **Protein:** 13.63 g | **Net Carbs:** 2.08 g | **Fat:** 19.26 g

Chicken Sausage Corn Dogs

Ingredients

4 links chicken sausage
1 ½ c. lard
1 c. almond flour
1 t. of each:
  -Ms. Dash Table Blend
  -Baking powder
½ t. of each:
  -Turmeric
  -Kosher salt
¼ t. cayenne pepper
2 large eggs
2 tbsp. heavy whipping cream
For the Pan: 1 ½ c. oil

Instructions

1. Combine the spices and almond meal. In another dish, whisk the heavy cream, egg, and

add the baking powder to the mixture.
2. Heat a saucepan with the oil (400° F).
3. Dip the dogs/sausages into the mixture and add them to the oil. Fry for approximately two minutes for each side.
4. Transfer to a plate of paper towels to drain. Add a stick to make it easy or enjoy from a serving platter.
5. Serve and enjoy!

Yields: 4 Low-Carb Corndogs

Calories: 493.75 | **Protein:** 15.4 g | **Net Carbs:** 4.52 g | **Fat:** 45.93 g

Corned Beef with Low-Carb Mustard Cream Sauce

Ingredients for the Corned Beef

5 lbs. pickled beef – approx. (70.55 oz.)
1 diced onion
3 garlic cloves
1 diced carrot
2 tbsp. olive oil
2 tbsp. lemon thyme
1 tbsp. whole peppercorns
4 ¼ c. beef stock – approx. (33.81 oz.)
¼ c. red wine vinegar
2 tbsp. salt
Also Needed: Pressure Cooker

Ingredients for the Mustard Cream Sauce

2 ½ oz. butter
1 ½ c. heavy cream

2 tbsp. Dijon mustard
1 t. pepper
1 pinch salt
1 tbsp. finely chopped parsley

Instructions

1. Rinse and pat dry the beef with a towel.
2. Saute the garlic, thyme, onion, and carrot in the oil using the high-heat setting for four minutes. Pour in the vinegar, peppercorns, and salt. Cook for two minutes and add the beef and stock along with just enough to cover the meat.
3. Tightly secure the lid on the slow cooker. Cook until the pot begins to release the steam. Lower the heat to low and cook for two hours – or - one hour for every 2.2 pounds of meat.
4. After two hours, turn off the heat and let the pressure release naturally (about 20 minutes). Remove the top, and lift out the beef with some tongs and a wooden spoon.
5. Prepare the sauce. In a small saucepan using low heat, combine the mustard and butter. Mix in the cream, but don't boil (It won't blend if it boils).
6. As the cream is reduced, the sauce will thicken by ½ of its volume. Blend in the pepper, salt, and parsley.
7. Slice the corned beef and drizzle with the sauce.

Notes: Pickled beef is submerged in brine for at least a week which replaces much of the natural meat juices. You can either discard the veggies and liquid or strain it to flavor soups later.

Yields: 12 Servings

Calories: 441| **Protein:** 22.8 g | **Net Carbs:** 1 g | **Fat:** 37.6 g

Hawaiian Hot Dogs - Open-Faced

Ingredients

2 c. shredded skim mozzarella cheese
½ c. fresh pineapple chunks
¾ c. almond flour
6 of each:
- -Jumbo all-beef hot dogs
- -Sarayo - Sriracha sauce
- -Chopped bacon slices
- -Ham slices

Instructions

1. Prepare the oven until it reaches 350° F. Line a baking tin with some parchment paper.
2. Melt the cheese over medium heat in a skillet, and stir in the flour to form a dough. Roll it out until flat between two pieces of parchment paper.
3. Cut out six circles and place them in the prepared pan. Bake for ten minutes.
4. When done, add the dog in the middle and

wrap it in the warm bread. Top with the ham, bacon, and pineapple. Add other toppings as desired, but add the carbs.

Yields: 6 Servings

Calories: 512.17| **Protein:** 24.93 g | **Net Carbs:** 7.62 g | **Fat:** 41.7 g

Chapter 7: Snacks –Appetizers & Dips

Snacks

Coconut Cashew Protein Bars – No-Bake

Ingredients

1 1/3 c. (4 scoops) protein powder
½ c. coconut butter
¼ c. of each:
  -Cashew butter
  -Coconut oil
2/3 c. ground flaxseed
¼ c. coconut/cashew milk
½ t. liquid stevia coconut drops
Optional Topping: Unsweetened coconut flakes
Also Needed: 8x8-inch baking dish

Instructions

1. Soften the coconut butter, cashew butter, and coconut oil in the microwave/saucepan. Stir to incorporate and set aside to cool.
2. In another container, whisk the flaxseed and protein powder. Stir in the milk.
3. Taste test the cashew/coconut mixture for sweetness and adjust accordingly. Combine the fixings, mixing well.

Yields: 12 Servings

Calories: 212 | **Protein:** 11.2 g | **Net Carbs:** 8.3 g | **Fat:** 16.2 g

Keto Bites - Grilled Ham & Cheese

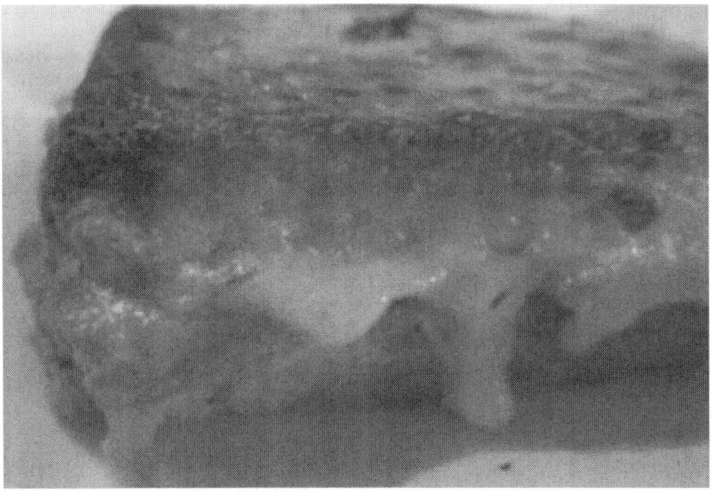

Ingredients for the Low-Carb Mini Buns

1 t. baking powder
¾ c. almond flour
¼ t. salt
2 tbsp. coconut oil
1 ½ tbsp. salted butter
2 large eggs
1 t. coconut flour

Ingredients for the Grilled Ham & Cheese

4 slices deli ham
1 tbsp. salted butter
2 slices of each:
  -Muenster cheese
  -Cheddar cheese
3 pieces - low-carb mini buns

Instructions for the Bread

1. Set the oven temperature to 350° F.
2. Combine the baking powder, almond flour, and salt.
3. In a small container, measure out the coconut oil and butter. Melt 20 seconds, and combine with the dry ingredients. Blend well to form a dough.
4. Scramble two eggs and add it to the dough. Add the coconut flour to thicken, and add to a muffin tin. Fill each one about ¾-inches full.
5. Bake until browned for about 18-20 minutes.
6. Let them cool about 10-15 minutes before moving from the pan.
7. Slice each one in half for the sandwich bun.

Instructions for the Sandwich

1. Warm the meat in a frying pan and stack the cheese (alternating pattern). Slice into quarters.
2. Arrange the cheese and ham between the buns.
3. Heat the butter on the med-high setting and arrange the sandwiches in the pan. Lower the heat to med-low. Flip and continue cooking until browned on both sides. Serve and enjoy.

Yields: 3 mini-grilled ham and cheese & 8 miniature low-carb buns

Calories: 235.25 | **Protein:** 9.38 g | **Net Carbs:** 1.85 g | **Fat:** 21.26 g

Avocado Ranch Dip

Ingredients

1 ripe med. avocado
1/3 c. plain non-fat yogurt
½ c. coconut/avocado oil mayonnaise
2 tbsp. freshly chopped of each:
- Parsley
- Dill

1 t. Worcestershire sauce
1 minced clove of garlic
¼ t. of each:
- Salt
- Onion powder
- Black pepper

½ t. of each:
- Smoked paprika
- White vinegar

Instructions

1. Mix all of the fixings in a food processor. Blend until smooth, scraping the sides as needed.
2. Taste and add spices to your liking. Store in an air-tight jar for one to two days.

Yields: 4 Servings – ¼ cup each

Calories: 171 | **Protein:** 1.1 g | **Net Carbs:** 1.4 g | **Fat:** 17.8 g

Krista's Queso in the Slow Cooker

Ingredients

1 pkg. (16 oz.) of each:
-Processed cheese food – cubed
-Bulk pork breakfast sausage
1 can diced tomatoes - green chile peppers (ex. Ro*Tel - 14 oz.)
1 jar (4 oz.) mushrooms
Also Needed: 1 Skillet

Instructions

1. Use the medium heat setting to warm up a pan. Prepare the sausage until browned, and drain.
2. Mix the rest of the ingredients in a slow cooker. Set the temperature to low for 30-40 minutes. Serve and enjoy.

Yields: 24 Servings

Calories: 153 | **Net Carbs:** 1.3 g | **Fat:** 13.5 g | **Protein:** 6.6 g

Sausage and Cheese Dip in the Slow Cooker

Ingredients

¼ c. sliced green onions
1 can (15 oz.) Ro*Tel hot diced tomatoes with Habaneros
1 lb. hot Italian ground sausage
8 oz. of each:
- Cream cheese
- Diced pepper jack cheese

16 oz. sour cream

Instructions

1. Prepare the sausage in a saucepan using the medium heat setting until browned lightly. Pour in the tomatoes and simmer about five minutes. Stir in the onions, and stop cooking once the sausage is browned for serving.
2. Layer the bottom of a slow cooker on the high setting with the pepper jack and cream cheese (in chunks). Add the sausage and spread out

the sour cream on the top.
3. Cook about one hour, stir the dip until well mixed. Continue cooking for a total of about two hours.

Yields: 28 Servings

Calories: 144 | **Protein:** 5.61 g | **Net Carbs:** 2.47 g | **Fat:** 12.19 g

Chapter 8: Dressings & Syrup

Salad Dressings

5-Minute Vinaigrette

Ingredients

35 drops liquid stevia
½ c. of each:
- Extra-virgin olive oil
- White wine vinegar
- Golden raspberries

Instructions

1. Use an immersion blender if you have one; if not, combine all of the ingredients in a mixing dish and blend well.
2. Strain the seeds out of the vinaigrette, and you are done.

Yields: 1 ½ c. Servings – 2 tbsp. each

Calories: 84 | **Protein:** 0.06 g | **Net Carbs:** 0.29 g | **Fat:** 9.03 g

Creamy Avocado Cilantro Lime Dressing

Ingredients

1 peeled garlic clove
1 avocado
3 tbsp. olive oil
¼ c. of each:
 -Greek yogurt/low-fat sour cream
 -White vinegar/fresh lime or lemon juice
¼ t. of each:
 -Freshly cracked black pepper
 -Kosher salt
Water
Also Recommended: Food processor or blender

Instructions

1. Process all of the fixings with the blender of choice until creamy smooth.
2. Thin the dressing out with approximately 1/3 cup of water until it's the desired texture.
3. Store in an air-tight container for one to two weeks.

Yields: 16 Servings -1 cup (1 tbsp. each)

Calories: 46 | **Protein:** 0.5 g | **Net Carbs:** 1.5 g | **Fat:** 4.4 g

Ginger Vinaigrette Dressing

Ingredients

3 tbsp. of each:
- -Soy sauce
- -Rice wine vinegar

1 packet stevia sweetener
1 tbsp. ginger
2 tbsp. sesame oil
½ t. garlic
½ c. peanut oil
1 tbsp. of each:
- -Toasted sesame seeds
- -Chopped scallion

Instructions

1. Use a food processor/whisk to combine the garlic, soy sauce, ginger, sweetener, and wine vinegar.
2. Whisk and slowly add the oils. Combine well and add the scallions and seeds.
3. Chill in the fridge and use within a week.

Yields: 10 Servings

Calories: 150 | **Protein:** 2 g | **Net Carbs:** 6 g | **Fat:** 14 g

Maple Syrup

Ingredients

1 tbsp. unsalted butter
2 ¼ t. coconut oil
¼ c. erythritol
¼ t. xanthan gum
¾ c. water
2 t. maple extract
½ t. vanilla extract
½ t. cinnamon – optional

Instructions

1. Combine the xanthan gum, coconut oil, and butter in a microwavable container. Cook 40-50 seconds.
2. Grind the erythritol until fine and mix with the oils and water.
3. Stir in the stevia along with the maple and vanilla extract. Add small amounts of water until it's the way you love it. Place in the microwave for 40 to 60 seconds.

4. Use when needed.

Yields: 4 Servings – 1 cup each

Calories: 56 | **Protein:** 0.03 g | **Net Carbs:** 0.34 g | **Fat:** 5.39 g

Chapter 9: Desserts

Anytime you want a tasty treat, try one of these!

Brownie Muffins

Ingredients

½ t. salt
1 c. flaxseed meal
¼ c. cocoa powder
1 tbsp. cinnamon
½ tbsp. baking powder
1 t. vanilla extract
2 tbsp. coconut oil
1 large egg
¼ c. of each:
 -Sugar-free caramel syrup
 -Silvered almonds
½ c. pumpkin puree
1 t. apple cider vinegar

Instructions

1. Program the oven temperature to 350° F.
2. In a mixing bowl, combine all of the fixings. Stir well.
3. Use six paper liners in the muffin tin, and pour ¼ cup batter into each one.
4. Sprinkle several almonds on the tops, pressing gently.
5. Bake approximately 15 minutes when the tops of the muffins are set.

Yields: 6 Servings

Calories: 183 | **Protein:** 7 g | **Net Carbs:** 3.3 g | **Fat:** 13.4 g

Coconut Chia Bars

Ingredients

½ c. water
4 tbsp. chia seeds
1 tbsp. each:
  -Coconut oil
  -Confectioners Swerve
1 c. shredded –dried - unsweetened- coconut meat
½ c. cashews
¼ t. vanilla extract

Instructions

1. Program the oven temperature to 350° F.
2. Soak the seeds for about 15 minutes until they become 'gel-like.' Combine with the coconut, oil, swerve, and vanilla extract.
3. Lastly, add the cashews. Line the mixture, using parchment paper, on a (9x9) cookie sheet. Press until it is about a ¾-inch thickness. Bake for 45 minutes.
4. It's done when tested with a toothpick in the center and comes out clean. Slice into six pieces and enjoy!

Yields: 6 Bars

Calories: 164 | **Protein:** 4 g | **Net Carbs:** 3.5 g | **Fat:** 14 g

Mocha Cheesecake Bars

Ingredients for the Brownie Layer

3 large eggs
6 tbsp. unsalted butter
2 t. vanilla extract
1 ½ c. almond flour
½ c. Hershey's Baking Cocoa
1 c. erythritol
½ t. salt
½ tbsp. instant coffee
1 t. baking powder

Ingredients for the Cream Cheese Layer

½ c. erythritol
1 large egg
1 lb. softened cream cheese
1 t. vanilla extract
Also Needed: 8x8-inch baking pan

Instructions

1. Program the oven to 350° F. Lightly grease/spray the pan.
2. Combine the wet fixings - starting with the vanilla and butter. Stir in the eggs.
3. In another container, combine the dry ingredients and whisk with the wet fixings. Set aside ¼ cup of the batter for later. Pour the mixture into the pan.
4. Mix the cream cheese (room temperature) with the rest of the ingredients for the second layer. Spread it on the sheet of brownies.
5. Use the reserved batter as the last layer (will be thin). Bake 30-35 minutes. When cooled, slice the cheesecake bars, and enjoy.

Yields: 16 Servings

Calories: 232 | **Protein:** 6.12 g | **Net Carbs:** 3.24 g | **Fat:** 21.15 g

Ultimate Crème Brûlée

Ingredients

5 egg yolks
2 c. heavy cream
1 pinch – salt
6 tbsp. erythritol – ex. Sukrin natural sweetener
1 whole vanilla bean
3 tbsp. powdered erythritol

Instructions

1. Preheat the oven and arrange six baking dishes in a large roasting pan. Also, bring a pot of water to boiling.
2. Combine ½ of the erythritol and cream in a medium saucepan. Split the vanilla bean lengthwise. Scrape the seeds into the pan. Use the medium setting to warm the fixings or about seven minutes.
3. Whisk the egg yolks with the salt and rest of erythritol. Use an electric mixer to combine

until it is pale yellow.

4. Use a spoon to add the hot cream mixture to the yolk. Combine only a spoonful at a time until the ingredients are well mixed. Use a strainer to remove the vanilla pods and cooked egg bits.
5. Empty the custard into the prepared dishes, adding water to go ½ way up the sides of the bowls.
6. Bake approximately 35 minutes or until set – but not too firm. Cover overnight for best results or a minimum of two hours.
7. Before serving sprinkle ½ tablespoon of the powdered erythritol over each dish. Use a torch or the oven broiler to caramelize the top. It must remain cold after torched. Rest a couple of minutes before enjoying.

Yields: 6 Servings

Calories: 320| **Protein:** 3.9 g | **Net Carbs:** 3.9 g | **Fat:** 31.4 g

Vanilla Bean Cupcakes

Ingredients for the Batter

2 large eggs
½ c. mayonnaise
1 tbsp. vanilla bean paste
½ c. erythritol
1 ¾ c. almond flour
¼ t. salt
2 t. baking powder

Ingredients for the Frosting

¼ c. powdered erythritol
4 oz. cream cheese
½ t. vanilla extract
3 tbsp. heavy whipping cream

Instructions

1. Set the oven temperature to 350° F.
2. Combine the bean paste, mayonnaise, and eggs in a mixing bowl. A hand mixer is helpful. Set it to the side once it is smooth.
3. In another container, combine the baking powder, salt, erythritol, and flour. Slowly, whisk the batter into the flour.
4. Add the batter (1/4 c. each) into the eight paper-lined muffin tins.
5. Bake for 20-25 minutes or until lightly browned. After cooled, add the frosting.

Yields: 8 Servings

Calories: 329| **Protein:** 7.7 g | **Net Carbs:** 4.2 g | **Fat:** 30.8 g

Conclusion

Thanks for reading your entire copy of the *Ketogenic Diet the Complete Beginner's Guide to Burn Fat and to Eat and Feel Healthy*. Let's hope it was informative and provided you with all of the tools you need to achieve your goals of burning away fat and feeling healthy. As you now see, you do not have to deprive yourself!

Here are a few unfortunate choices made by dieters as reasons that could cause your diet to fail. Making adjustments to your lifestyle doesn't need to become a dreaded task - if you plan the route to success ahead of meal times

You learn from your mistakes, and these are some of the ones that can happen along the path:

Mistake One: Dining by the Clock: Just because the clock says it is 12:00 noon or 6:00 dinnertime doesn't mean you must have a meal. If you have in the past, you understand the pitfall. One crucial step while you are dieting is that you should never eat unless you are hungry. Take the clues from your body, not the clock.

Mistake Two: Dieting Solo: Dieting is a challenge, but many individuals have discovered dieting with another friend, or family members can make the task seem less stressful. Many of the temptations can be removed if everyone is on the same page. You can also join a support group online or better yet – start your own team. The primary element is to be around individuals who understand your struggle. Praise of losing the pounds and inches while staying healthy is what the Keto diet plan is all about!

Mistake Three: Becoming Obsessed with the Weighing Scales: Weighing often can sometimes cause setbacks, because you don't believe you are progressing as fast as you want to at this point. You have to realize the numbers you are viewing on the scales are from work done previously; not today. Your weight will fluctuate daily according to your water weight, so it is not as dependable as waiting for a week or more before you weigh.

Mistake Four: Obsessing Over the Macros: The keto diet plan takes a lot of the stress out of the process of counting the macros. It is a simple process to track the numbers but try not to become obsessed with them.

Mistake Five: Lack of Commitment: You have to be ready to change your lifestyle and become determined to eat for your health. You have to commit yourself 100% to the plan to reap the promising results. Only you know how many grams of food you have consumed in one day. Be honest when recording your intake amounts.

Mistake Six: Lack of Essential Nutrients: According to the experts, you need to be getting salt in your diet daily. You need to consume a minimum of two teaspoons each day, as well as Vitamin D and magnesium while on the keto plan. Many of the nutrients are supplied through your foods.

Mistake Seven: Eating the Wrong Types of Fat: You need to steer clear of seed and vegetable oils (many stored in plastic containers). Instead, purchase saturated fats such as butter, animal fats, or coconut oil, and monounsaturated fat such as olive oil, and fish oil.

Mistake Eight: Consuming Too Much Protein: Protein provides an essential macro essential to building your muscles, organs, and other soft tissues. Your efforts to reach ketosis will be sabotaged if you consume too much protein. If you eat more than you need, the surplus will be transformed into glucose.

Mistake Nine: Comparison to Others: The success of this diet plan depends on what you believe is right and correct, not what others think is right. Everyone gains and loses weight differently; it isn't a one-size-fits-all situation. Just because a friend lost 30 pounds in 30 days, and you didn't; doesn't make you a failure. It merely means you have to become more diligent and try again.

Finally, if you found this book useful in any way, a review on Amazon is always appreciated! Happy Cooking!

If you enjoy such content, do subscribe to our nonfiction readers list where we feature great content, give FREE books every now and then and also give valuable tips that you can use in your life! Generally, a great place for nonfiction readers to hang out!

Click here -> http://eepurl.com/c5bzdX

Do check out my other books that helps you become healthier as well!

Burn Fat: Understand & End Obesity Once And For All

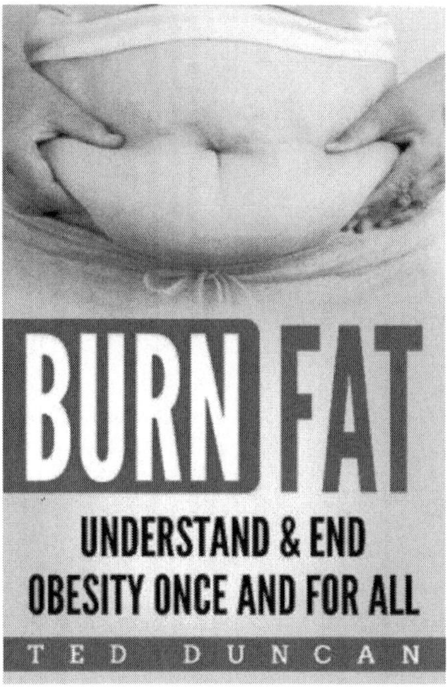

The Keto Crockpot - Effective Weight Loss Recipes To Burn Fat 10x Faster Eating Delicious Foods

27695004R00079

Printed in Great Britain
by Amazon